D0874479

DIAMOND MIND

How to Gain Clarity and Strength
Through the Pressure of Life's Obstacles

Learn more about the Diamond Mind authors at diamondmindbook.com

TABLE OF CONTENTS

INTRODUCTION

You were born with a light inside of you.

Your talents, aspirations, hopes, dreams, strengths, and all the uniqueness that is you is yearning to get out and shine bright. But somewhere along the road of life, darkness started to creep in and dim your light.

What is holding YOU back from your highest potential?

In *Diamond Mind*, ten empowered women share their individual stories of struggle and triumph. Because just like you, they have faced stressors, hardships, and tragedies. And in these pages, you'll learn not only how they were able to overcome, but how these struggles made them more powerful and persevering.

Just like a diamond, it is the pressure that initiates transformation into clarity and strength.

You have the power to:

Choose courage over fear.

Turn your mess into your message.

Step into the powerful woman you're destined to be.

It's time to let your light shine. *Diamond Mind* will show you the way.

CHAPTER ONE

THE MAGIC OF BEING IN TOUCH WITH YOUR INTUITION

By Marilys Candelario

What if I told you that the universe is always conspiring to give you everything your heart desires? Could I get you to believe me?

When was the last time you wanted something and couldn't get it off your mind?

Ever have a test you weren't ready for get rescheduled?

Or a meeting you didn't want to attend get postponed?

How about you run into some unexpected money only to cover an unexpected cost?

Even something as simple as the person you have been

thinking of calling you, it could be a coincidence, or it could be the universe granting your heart's desires.

On the contrary, ever not follow your gut instinct on something? How did that feel? Were you upset with yourself for not listening?

The clarity to know better, or do better, tends to be gained in retrospect. Grab a journal and let's get you started on the journey back to yourself.

And listen ... with enough mindful intentional thinking, the answers will arrive, don't quit just because the answers don't come easily. This is the whole point, without clarity you can't awaken from within.

Journal Prompt 1: What do I need to let go of? What am I ready to let go of? What am I tired of reliving over and over again? What is stopping me from acting in my best interest? What narrative do I keep repeating?

At times, what might be stopping us is **our inner dialogue**. The **constant narrative** I always heard in my mind was, "you have to be successful. Your teen mom did not give up her youth in vain, a lot is expected of you."

Due to that narrative, my definition of success has continued to evolve over time. Each goal I achieved throughout my life helped me realize I did not "feel" different. I did not feel more accomplished because I met some of the goals that I thought would deem me successful. There is a misconception of what it means to have it all, how it must feel to be strong, how strength is measured, and what it takes to have the vision to pursue your passion.

Beware! You can have it all and not feel in control of your life. You can be strong and be extremely unhappy. Strength is measured by the ability to be in alignment with inner wisdom.

Pursuing your soul's purpose with passion takes sacrifice. I have had to release my desires to spontaneously travel, limit my spending, release relationships that don't serve me and calculate my time with extreme caution. At times this feels suffocating.

In my early 20's I was **repeating the same mistakes** especially when it came to external validation of love.

I was always hoping to win over someone, especially if they underestimated me. I would journal and ask myself…

Why are you always looking for attention?

Why don't you stop talking to people who don't treat you right?

The lessons that you don't learn will continue to show up.

I wonder when I stopped listening to my gut?

Letting Go and Unlearning

If I held onto the following ideals I would never have unlearned all the lessons that created the barrier between myself and my instincts:

"If too many obstacles present themselves then you are going against the current and should relax and let it all come to you."

"Just be a nice girl, no one likes an angry loud girl."

"Do unto others as you'd like done to you", aka the "golden rule".

I have a pet peeve with the Golden Rule because it creates a lot of expectations of others that, in most circumstances, will continuously go unfulfilled. It put me in this vicious cycle that I should treat others - rather than myself- how I want to be treated. I was not taught to say no because, whether intentionally or unintentionally, I picked up that saying no is rude. These important initial lessons in life created a foundation for future painful hardships. I began to peel back the layers in the unlearning and that led me to begin building trust within myself.

What does it mean to intuitively trust yourself? Trust is built upon 3 pillars:

1. Competence: you are good at what you do

2. Reliability: you do what you say you will

3. Kindness: you have the best interest at heart

***Journal Prompt 2*:** Does trusting myself feel impossible? What will make me commit to the process? How can I **make medicine from my hardships**?

My journal entry around this topic looked a little bit like this:

In 2016, giving birth to my daughter and committing to breastfeeding, through all the hurdles that presented themselves, is how I "made my medicine". I have no control over what obstacles will present themselves in her life, but I can raise her to trust her instincts. That meant leading by example. For starters, I needed to believe I am a good mom no matter how hard the voice in my head screamed that I could do better. I follow through on the tough discipline when it would be much simpler to cave. I reevaluate what our family's best interest looks like each day and connect to my kids and husband with the kindness and respect I give to strangers. That is how I practice intuitively trusting myself within motherhood and within my marriage.

When you are about to **begin a new chapter of your life**, some people may not believe you, some may not recognize your shift, and some boundaries will be necessary to protect your progress. Keep that in mind and check in periodically to ensure your inner circle is lighting your path rather than igniting a flame. Don't be scared to be #TeamNewFriends.

Start Small

Baggage. BOOM! In case you didn't know already, we all have some of it! Sometimes it is old baggage we haven't unpacked. Other times it is the present baggage we have not processed. Most times it is something we can see, feel, and recognize needs attention. But most times we prefer to let it be our crutch. Our "reason" we can't be loved.

Journal Prompt 3: Take a moment to reflect on and list your obstacles below.

My obstacles are: I was born to a teenage mother, father was not present due to distance, alcoholic dysfunctional home, and sexual harassment experiences... Your turn...

Start Simple

Have faith and hope that you can overcome anything. Mind over matter, mindfulness is key. Pick an obstacle above and see if you can begin to reframe an element of your narrative to have a positive spin.

Start Now

Time is currency = put it towards the things that yield what you want to see. Rearrange your time appropriately, and drop the idea that there aren't enough hours in a day - do you think Beyonce & Oprah let the hours in a day limit their greatness?

With time, confidence will emerge. "Success is not a destination that you ever reach, **success is the quality of your journey.**" One small simple step you can take right now - even if you did not complete the prompt above is learning to be empathetic. You can start by removing all the trash you intake. Whether that is trashy tv, social media accounts, or toxic people. If you can't remove a toxic person then build a boundary.

Stressful Much?

When you change the relationship you have with stress it can be the magic sauce to change things for you. As my relationship with stress has evolved, I've noticed that stress is supposed to be beneficial. In positive amounts, it is what pushes you to keep striving to overcome obstacles. I don't think people are aware that they are in a relationship with stress and therefore able to change the dynamics of that relationship.

Journal Prompt 4: Take a moment to reflect on how you interact with the stress that presents itself both externally and internally.

We are perpetually facing obstacles that create enormous amounts of stress. When that stress starts to get out of control it leaks out in a variety of ways. Instead of labeling it as a response to stress and assessing an action plan to release that stress in a healthy way, we let it keep compounding and internalize it.

Let's identify if you have a pattern of physical symptoms potentially caused by stress, check off the symptoms that apply below:

Low energy.

Headaches.

Digestive issues.

Aches, pains, and tension.

Rapid heartbeat.

Insomnia.

Frequent colds and infections.

For me, it is aches and canker sores. I experience canker sores when I am extremely stressed. For a long time, I had a negative connotation to stress and thought stress meant being frustrated, angry, or upset. Sometimes I'm really happy and get a lot of canker sores, and I'm like why? You can be stressed even when you are happy. The sores are my body's way of communicating that I need to rest.

Safe Coping Mechanism: During this time if you feel triggered you can process your emotions in the following way:

Label them. Respond to them. Don't internalize them.

The key is to recognize the inner dialogue so you can label it. Mine goes something like this, "you can't handle it all, you aren't good enough, just give up". I recognize the voice and actively respond by muting it and replacing it with an affirmation or a mantra. I like to use:

"I radiate positive energy"

"Life on the other side of anger is more joyous"

"I am full of light and love"

"I accept the healing I unconsciously seek"

When all else fails I go out for a walk and try to be with nature or just rage clean my bathroom. I urge you to find ways to **release that stress** - recognize when it's getting the best of you and release it.

Before I had all these coping mechanisms in place, I struggled. It was hard to speak openly to my partner about my experiences. I felt a loss of identity and felt out of touch. I battled myself for so long because I was fighting against an inner dialogue telling me life shouldn't be this hard, that I shouldn't get frustrated with my kids. That I am ungrateful if I don't enjoy every minute of the day with them. I should not put myself down because of these thoughts. Once my inner dialogue shifted I was able to take care of myself on the outside.

How I Gained Clarity?

The next time you go shopping ask yourself: are you buying something because it is on sale or because you love it ... you love it so much you need to have it? Need is a very intricate word that is overused a lot. Do you need that coffee? That sale item? Or do you want it because you have been conditioned to believe your wants are needs? Practice identifying your needs. Over time you will have the capacity to recover quickly from difficulties since you will be in touch with your needs and by catering to them you build your inner strength and resilience. All those "wants" create more barriers on the journey back to yourself.

I leave you with this wish:

- Dream way bigger than a career, marriage, white picket fence, and/or kids. You are capable of so much more;

- Approach each and every day as if the universe is conspiring to give you everything your heart desires;

- Find ways to cleanse your energy and release all the negative energy of the experiences and people weighing you down; and

- When you feel ready, cut all ties to the negativity that surrounds you – be ruthless! Your peace and self-care should be prioritized above ALL else.

Love,

Mari

May my story of resilience stir up the controversy to get you started on your journey.

CHAPTER TWO

DREAM YOUR WAY OUT

By Michelle East-Walker

H ave you ever felt like your job is killing you? Well, my job literally was killing me from the inside out. I worked for a well-known fortune 500 financial company, and the environment was toxic. They threatened, bullied, recorded phone conversations, constantly tested compliance knowledge, and held surprise audits all with the intention of catching us doing something wrong. There was no safe space to work within this company, and because of the constant stress I was under, my body reacted by shutting down. A few years later, a class-action lawsuit would be filed against them, and I would receive a small sum of money as compensation for what they put me and others through.

But before we get too far into the story, let me tell you about myself. The loves of my life are my family, husband, children, and fur baby. In the early morning hours, you can find me in meditation with the sunrise, journaling my thoughts and plans for the day. I ask myself while sipping on a cup of hot tea and watching nature wake up, what is the most important thing for today. Subsequently, I transition into work mode with my Wall Street Journal and prepare for my job as a stock trader. In the evenings, unwinding means having a glass of wine with my husband and watching the sunset reflect upon the lake behind our home.

Yoga in some form has always been a part of my being. For me, the mat represents a sacred place to find solace and centering. I am grateful to have been trained as a 500-hour yoga and meditation teacher. This training has helped me immensely in navigating life's challenges, giving me a foundation to dream my way out and into a new life.

As a young impressionable girl, my grandmother Gloria set a course for my life, although I didn't know it at the time. Gloria grew up during the great depression, and like many of that generation, money was scarce. As an adult, she developed a passion for the stock market but financial careers for women were slim to none in those days. Being smart and determined, she didn't let that stop her. Instead, she educated herself about the market on her own and put her knowledge to use to become wealthy.

Following a path unavailable for my grandmother, I pursued finance as a career, earning a bachelor's and master's degree. I went on to obtain two federal licenses that allowed me to be a Stockbroker and Financial Advisor. That means I can sell you stocks and advise you about your investments.

While climbing the corporate ladder, I began to realize the trappings of corporate life were not worth the toll they were taking on my health. The demands of the job created stress. This stress sent me spiraling into a state of chronic fatigue syndrome, gastritis, hair loss, panic attacks, anxiety disorder, and high blood pressure coupled with a constant high heart rate. To this day, I am still under the care of a cardiologist in order to keep the long-term effects of stress under control.

I knew I had hit rock bottom while attending a company sales meeting for my job in Colorado. Things started off well enough. I flew from Florida into Denver and met up with old friends I knew within the company. However, the next day was a different story. As I watched the conference unfold and listened to all the corporate-speak, my heart rate became elevated. I had to leave the event and rest in my room.

The next morning, I woke and had a difficult time getting out of bed. My heart was racing again, and I was forced to constantly rest in between dressing and preparing for the day ahead. Already late, I quickly ate and entered the conference room to join the others. Once the presentation began, I knew I was not going to be able to participate.

I staggered out to the lobby, and the head of Human Resources found me. She inquired as to what was wrong, and I explained about my heart rate. She contacted the nurse for our company and one of the hotel staff that knew CPR. They asked if I wanted to go to the hospital. At that point, I knew I had to make an important decision. I either had to stay in Denver and be admitted to the hospital alone or try to make it home to Jacksonville, FL. I decided to go home. They booked me a flight, put me in an Uber, and sent me on my way alone. When I reached the airport, barely able to complete the security check-in, I looked back one last time at Colorado, which represented corporate America for me, and I said goodbye. I vowed to myself that I would never work for a large corporation again.

Using my yoga breathing techniques to keep my heart rate under control as much as possible, I survived the flight. Once I landed in Jacksonville, I was extremely disoriented and walking at a snail's pace. My husband met me with a wheelchair and rushed me to the ER, where I was admitted. With an IV in place, doctors performed many tests and I spent several days in a medicated fog. Drugs were used as a standard medical practice to stabilize the symptoms I was experiencing. However, I knew pills were not the answer. Without a doubt, I knew the only answer was to reframe my entire life.

Once able to leave the hospital, I immediately took medical leave combined with short-term disability. At first, my body would not allow me to do anything. Even getting myself to the restroom was a complete drain, so all I could do was rest. It was surreal. Everyone around me still had their same lives. My husband went to his job, my children attended school, friends had their normal routines. I was left alone staring at this blank canvas of my life, wondering what was to become of me.

Looking at the silver lining, I found that I had been given a gift of medical leave, which carved space in my life to begin the journey of holistic healing. In my home, I diffused essential oils to give me a sense of calm. Slowly, I tended to my herb garden, which gave me a quiet connection with life. Meditation became the only form of yoga available to me, and I realized the amazing benefits of calming my mind, controlling my breath, and focusing inward.

During this period of complete stillness, I began to journal. This practice of recording my feelings gave way to uninterrupted contemplation. Contemplation then gave way to complete clarity of what I needed to do. But clarity did not come without a fight. Fear from the past physical, emotional, and psychological trauma surfaced many times during this healing process. I was fearful about what the future would hold for me.

The struggle of finding one's self again and rebuilding a whole new life is not easy. I was emotionally overwhelmed, and an identity crisis brewed inside of me. I began to examine questions like who are we without the labels the world puts on us? Who would I be if I wasn't a stockbroker if I had no title? I sounded cool at parties with that title. I commanded a level of respect with that title. If I didn't work for a company, who was I? How could I support and contribute to my family without a 9-5 job?

Additional revelations surfaced as well. I had created a life of consumerism and comparison. Digging deep inside, I began to see the vision of what I wanted my new life to look like. A life designed with purpose and freedom. I created a dream board with pictures and words that manifested my inner desires. My mantra became "Tell me what it is you plan to do with your one wild and precious life?" a beautiful line by the poet Mary Oliver.

To make this envisioned life real, I had to come to a place of acceptance with my past. I peeled back layer upon layer of protection I had built up and found my own personal inner peace, relying on the strength to love myself for who I was without a title, without a 9-5 job. This change in me required immense trust in my intuition, the ability to claim my voice and the courage to rise.

Once my medical leave ended, I was mentally prepared to quit my job, and that is exactly what I did. Slowly weaning myself off all medications except for the heart medicine, I felt stronger and clearer. Physically, I was not one hundred percent, but I was well enough to begin to take some practical steps in the direction of my future. With the support of my loving husband, we began to simplify our lives, deciding what was important, setting goals, and gently removing what no longer resonated with our overall life plan.

Looking at my skillset from different angles, I realized I was capable of much more than I had been settling for. I could use my knowledge of the stock market in new ways. One reason I originally became a financial advisor was my love for encouraging and educating women in the field of investing. Immediately, one of the first actions I took was to create a podcast that I use as a platform to share my knowledge of finance to women all over the world.

Something else significant came to my awareness: I had always wanted to day trade stocks but never had the confidence. In the stock market, there is no ceiling of pay. I could create my own destiny without the confines of a corporate overseer. With the recognition of these new purposeful vocations, my husband set up an amazing office in our home. Letting go of past expectations of what I should be doing and embracing this amazing and fresh life process, I enrolled in an online stock educational and trading community. Over the next few months, I built a daily routine and fostered friendships with like-minded day traders. Now, I have created an income source based on trading stocks every day. Life no longer runs me; I have the freedom to learn, earn, and give back based entirely from my heart.

During this time, I decided to get my first tattoo: a lotus flower permanently inked on my back in between my shoulder blades at the base of my neck. The placement between my heart and throat chakras represents love and expression. The lotus is one of the most beautiful flowers in the world. It begins life in the mud at the bottom of a pond and rises to the surface to bloom. For me, it symbolizes the passage from life's obstacles to a place where our petals open one by one and we flourish beyond our wildest dreams.

I may not fit into the image you have in your head of a stock day trader; I like to think of myself as more of a Wall Street meets Woodstock kind of girl. Near my desk, you will find a salt lamp, an essential oil diffuser, and healing crystals. Conversations during my day can fluctuate between the seven chakra energy centers of the body and how the Dow Jones Industrial Average is moving. More than anything, I have come to a place of peace with who I am at my core without needing confirmation from anyone else.

My deepest desire is that you would receive the gift of the lotus flower. Rise from the mud of your past or current situation, claim your deepest dreams, and begin taking small steps as I did. This path can lead you towards loving yourself with kindness and compassion and becoming your own best friend. Most of all, believe in your self-worth, knowing you can reach new heights through the mud. Eventually, you will reveal the petals of your life opening beautifully one by one. This, my dear, will bring you self-satisfaction and true joy.

CHAPTER THREE
HOW TO RECALIBRATE YOUR LIFE

By Jessica DeBry

"I'm sorry ... but I don't see a heartbeat."

T he doctor looked at me with compassionate eyes as I slowly tried to digest the information. I felt sick. Nauseous and uneasy, I swallowed saliva as my stomach turned over like reaching the bottom of a triple rollercoaster loop.

No. Not like this. Not *me*, I thought to myself. Not my baby. This. Can't. Be. Real.

Just 24 hours earlier, my husband Wes and I were celebrating what was a momentous occasion for me: I had recently become a bestselling author. My book *She Creates the Way* climbed the charts on Amazon to reach #1 in two different categories during launch week. In addition, I had just reached my biggest subscriber month for the subscription box business that I founded the previous year, SHEclub Monthly. After past failed entrepreneurial endeavors, I was proud of myself for starting over and creating this new business that was a hit from the start.

But most of all, we were celebrating what we knew was going to be our greatest adventure of all: the birth of our first child. Although I was only two months into the pregnancy, we were both feeling the nervous, excited buzz of what was on the horizon.

We sat together in our favorite neighborhood Italian restaurant, clinking together our glasses (Chianti for him, Shirley Temple for me) and battling over the last piece of oily garlic bread, grinning as we shared our hopes and dreams for our baby. And although it took us countless months to get to this place, those months of trying felt like they were all worth it as we shared in our elation for this next chapter in our lives. As we drove home from the restaurant, Wes reached his hand across the console to grab mine, squeezing it tightly while whispering, "this is going to be amazing".

I smiled as I fell asleep that night, dreaming sweet dreams of the next day's ultrasound where I'd get to see my 8-week-old, tiny blueberry-sized little one for the first time. I had no idea that it would quickly turn into a nightmare.

The doctor said the words aloud and the reality hit me like a ton of bricks, "unfortunately, this is not a viable pregnancy. You will most likely miscarry within the next few days..." and everything else blurred together. All I could think about was that this beautiful growing being inside of me, the one that finally started to flourish after months and months of trying, my perfect 'Lil Blueberry ... was no longer.

Devastating is an understatement. If you are a woman who has experienced a miscarriage or pregnancy loss, you know what I mean when I say that it shakes you to your core. Hopes and dreams of the future are quickly yanked away and filled with emptiness. You grieve for something that will always be a part of you. And *you cry for what will never become.*

And even with all of the other positive things that had just happened in my life, this tragedy quickly washed all of those happy emotions away. It felt like a sad, cruel joke from the Universe, the feeling of "having it all" just barely in my hands before falling through my fingertips. In the height of my own business success in one moment, and facing a devastating personal loss the next.

I didn't know it at the time, but this personal hardship would inspire me to recalibrate my life.

After the tears slowed and the darkness gradually started to make way for light, a new horizon emerged (and yes, that included a rainbow baby!).

Here's what I know now...

You're stronger than you'll ever know.

You have the power to heal from your hardship.

There is meaning in your misfortune.

So if you're dealing with something right now, girl, *I know how you feel*. I've been there. Trust me when I tell you that perhaps this hardship is a gift that will help you recalibrate your life, transforming it into something else, whether that be something different or even something better than you've ever dreamed of.

It's time to...

Heal yourself.

Empower your life.

Create the future that you've always envisioned.

Ready to recalibrate?

Step One: Adopt (or Force) an Attitude of Gratitude

Believe me, I understand how silly and out-of-touch it may sound to "be grateful" when you're going through hell. I would've definitely chucked a glass of wine at someone if they would have told me to simply "make a gratitude list" when I was in the midst of going through my miscarriage.

This is why you gotta force it. Seriously. Politely coerce your mental energy into gratitude and I promise it'll pay off. Why? Because it's a shift. It may not change the circumstances, but even if for a brief moment, it alters your lens on life.

Forcing an attitude of gratitude became a safe avenue for me to channel my thoughts. I may not have been able to prevent the overwhelming weight of feeling the loss of a baby growing inside me, but for a few minutes, I could be grateful for a fresh cup of coffee mixed with my favorite sugary-sweet vanilla creamer, enjoyed while sitting on the couch with a purring cat in my lap. When I forced my mental and emotional energy into feeling grateful for these small moments and things, the bigger and more daunting things were metaphorically swept under the rug, allowing time to pass and healing to come in.

Think about things, small or big, that are bringing you joy at this very moment. Aim for at least ten. Breathe deeply, channel your energy, and let the gratitude feeling wash over you as you revel in these beautiful things in your life.

Step Two: Take Inventory

Every retail establishment, restaurant, and business has a process for taking inventory. They track what's currently on hand and what needs to be replaced, in addition to charting what's getting them their best ROI, and what needs to be placed on clearance because ain't nobody gonna buy THAT weird thing so *it's gotta go ASAP.*

Businesses know the importance of taking inventory. So why aren't we doing it in our personal lives? Knowing what's working and what's not is especially crucial during a time of change or growth.

Going through a miscarriage reinforced my yearning to have a child (something that I previously wasn't sure about). But it also forced me to reevaluate everything else in my life. Now that my raw emotions were laid bare with my pregnancy loss, I became super clear with my emotions everywhere else.

I reevaluated the stuff that I previously thought was well and good and "working". The big thing here was my subscription box business. Whereas it was profitable and on an upwards growth trajectory, it was taking up a huge portion of my time and causing constant stress. Put bluntly, I simply *wasn't happy* about it anymore. I felt, deep in my bones, that by following on the path of this business I was walking further and further away from the pathway of having a child. Sometimes it takes a devastating personal experience to make your priorities crystal clear. I knew what I had to do: say goodbye to it and move on.

What's currently working for you? More importantly ... what's *not* working for you? Take inventory of your life so that you can make the appropriate changes moving forward.

Step Three: Build a Temporary Bridge

How do you get from Point A to Point B if there's a huge gaping ravine between the two? Simple: build a temporary bridge.

So many of us get so caught up in trying to plan out the perfect next steps to take that we're stuck in analysis paralysis. We're living in No Action Land, doing Google searches on exactly how to map out our scenario and watching hours of Youtube videos on the subject. Meanwhile, time is passing by and we're still nowhere close to getting what we actually want.

Let me be completely clear about something. You don't need a perfect bridge. You need a temporary one. Stop trying to make everything perfect before you take action! Stop the Google searches, stop the Youtube videos. *You'll never have a perfect pathway.* Instead, create something temporary that can tide you over while you figure everything else out.

Once it was crystal clear that I knew I needed to close my business, the next hurdle arose: money. I briefly contemplated starting a different business but knew that in doing so, I was delaying the inevitable *one thing* that I knew needed to focus on (creating, growing, and birthing a baby). So I got a job with the sole intention of having it pay my bills while I personally focused on getting pregnant. After years of being my own boss, it was a very strange transition to be working for someone else again (note to self: back-to-back Monday morning team meetings are bad for the soul). While I diligently showed up in the office in exchange for a paycheck that was just a fraction of my previous business earnings, I reminded myself that this was temporary for getting to where I actually wanted to be. Was it selfish to take a job knowing that it was temporary? Maybe. But we all have different intentions for things that we do. And at the end of the day, you have to put yourself and your own needs and wants first.

Build a temporary bridge. Remind yourself that it is exactly that: temporary. And as the pathway unfolds itself, you'll forget about the bridge itself and channel your focus into what that bridge is getting you to (hint: that thing you've always wanted *and* your dream life!).

Step Four: Trust Your Timing

I'll keep this short and sweet: *You are exactly where you're supposed to be.*

There's a reason why you are here, at this exact moment. Trust yourself, trust the Universe, and trust your timing as you move forward in this next chapter in your life.

Step Five: Let the Dots Connect Themselves

"You can't connect the dots looking forward; you can only connect them looking backwards. So you have to trust that the dots will somehow connect in your future. You have to

trust in something — your gut, destiny, life, karma, whatever.
This approach has never let me down, and it has made all
the difference in my life." - Steve Jobs

A funny thing happened shortly after I went all-in on
recalibrating my life: everything fell into place. It almost
seemed *too* easy.

Not to get all cliché on you here, but it's important to
emphasize something in case you haven't experienced it yet,
and that's the *power of intention.* Because once you make
your intention known, and start taking action to get there, the
pathway unfolds with ease. The Universe guides you
forward. And the dots connect as you look back. I say this,
not as a stereotypical cheesy airy-fairy thing, but as a holy-
crap-it-actually-works-and-I'm-living-proof-of-it thing.

After months of emotional healing from my miscarriage
(while forcing an attitude of gratitude) and making the tough
decision to close a profitable business to focus on getting
pregnant, I got a job, and *just one week later* I was pregnant
again. Keep in mind, this was something that previously took
my husband and me over 13 consistent months of trying.
Then, like magic from the Universe, a few weeks after that,
I had a wild idea for a new business. I quit that job and
launched a self-publishing consulting company that lit me up

from the inside out by empowering other women to share their stories with the world. Everything fell into place. I had metaphorically given birth to a new, passionate business endeavor and was just about to give actual physical birth to a baby boy.

That was almost a year ago. Now, as I sit here typing this in my home office, I have a baby monitor on my right (with little man sleeping peacefully) and an exciting business to-do list on my left. I squeeze in work time during baby's naps and early mornings, and I simultaneously have so much love for the little man *and* so much passion for my business.

It's not all rainbows and sunshine. This is real life - of course there are good moments and bad. But it all makes sense now. All is in alignment. I am so thankful for this journey as I would not be here without it (another cliché, I know! But it's oh so true).

You can't see the future before it happens. But you *can* grab hold of the present and make the choice to recalibrate.

No matter what you're facing, your time is now. Everything is possible.

Trust your timing and let the dots connect themselves. Because they always do.

CHAPTER FOUR

EMBRACING HEALING

By Katrina Turner

I remember sitting in my car, shaking. What the hell was I going to do? I was a 22-year-old mom of two. At the age 97% of my friends were finishing college, binge drinking, or traveling, I was about to take in two little girls and be in charge of them. Me, the girl who outdrank guys on multiple occasions and had a true passion for cheetah print and ripped jeans was now supposed to somehow navigate these two angels thru the most traumatic season of their lives. *help emoji*

Trauma. What an incredible word. What an incredible meaning. Coming in as a small-minded know-it-all, I am now constantly learning as much as possible of how we all connect to trauma. I started uncovering trauma my friends and I brushed off and related it to so many downfalls and feelings of negative self-worth.

I had the natural privilege of a mediocre life. Middle-class family, no crazy traumatic events, and a generally boring, yet beautiful childhood. So, trauma to me was what I read about in news articles after a car crash or something. I never really related to it or even made sense of it. So, imagine the world of shock as I entered foster care. Every child I held had a crippling backstory that eventually got so unsettling I had recurring nightmares. I was having debilitating panic attacks and would use the hours where they were sleeping to educate myself on everything I could.

What if you can't get over giving that child back? This is the most prominent response I get as a foster parent. What if that hurt lasts forever and eats us alive? I get it. I'm not immune to the pain just because I understand it. It sucks doing what's best for a child you love as your own. It is one of the most selfless things I have ever done. I'm picturing a very specific babe as I'm typing this and can feel warm tears flood my face. The connection and growth and strength she has makes me so proud. And missing her is an obstacle I jump over with every memory.

But what about all the life we live faced with loss every day due to death or addiction? Seeing someone you love lay in a coffin causes so much hurt and love and pain. It is, unfortunately, something most of us have to experience in this life. What about a toxic relationship? If you tell me that, as a woman, you have never been in one, I am SO happy for you. I have so many women of so many ages struggling with who they are because of some guy they thought the world of.

And thinking of all this made my heart stop, and I came to the realization that society thinks it can put a value on our trauma. That is not okay. It is not a ranking system. It's not a competition or something you're not allowed to heal from because everyone else has it worse. It's not your fault. It's not that bad. And it sure as hell is not meant to be ignored.

WE ARE ALLOWED TO FEEL AND HURT. WE ARE ALLOWED TO HEAL.

Trauma that happened to you, in whatever form, for whatever reason, is not to be compared. It is to be healed. It's not this anchor holding you back from all these incredibly beautiful things in your life. Trauma is so much more delicate and complex than what society tells us it is. It is so much more than just a word to describe something bad effecting us that we don't want to talk about. I truly, with all my heart, believe the key to a more freeing life as a powerful woman is discovering and healing from trauma in any way you decide.

Healing is thrown around in the world today. I believe in therapy, but also therapy in nature. I believe in breaks from alcohol, in learning something new, and doing something scary. I did a complete soul search. I read books that spoke to me. I traveled alone. I pursued an education in yoga. Those worked, but they worked because, for the first time, I was paying attention to me and what was good for me.

As a woman, I have to be careful not to get sucked into the online world. I can't look at Instagram and see aesthetically pleasing girls and get obsessed with copying that. I can't be a Pinterest mom. I tend to see all of these things and put it ahead of who I really am. I want to be nothing but authentically me. No ifs, ands, or buts. And when I picture and explore that woman, I find all the things that serve her. That heal her. And it is such a beautiful process.

So, see your trauma and be ready to face it, as a woman who knows who she is. Society will try to define you, but you don't have to let them. You are not just (I HATE THE WORD JUST) a foster kid, and you're not a slut or a homewrecker. What hurts you isn't a permission slip for people to call you crazy or belittle your emotions. The great thing about healing is you can honestly pick YOUR values, YOUR interests, and YOUR successes. Your wins are precious little hugs to yourself. Remember that.

About a month after our first placement, this little girl was screaming for her mom. She wondered why she wasn't "good enough" for her. I sat down and looked her dead in the eye. I wiped tears with the edges of my hoodie sleeves. My words exactly were: "You are so enough that it gives me chills." It was like it wasn't even me speaking. Some voice came over me, and I felt such a spiritual surge of complete love and strength.

That moment stays with me because I envision myself as that little girl. My inner child. And I am so enough that it hurts, and so was she, and so was her mom, and so are you.

Things happen in your life that are incredibly hurtful and unfair. Sometimes, they will almost break you. But you have a choice. You can take them on with the weight of hurtful things that people have said or done to you, or you can be a full-blown force of a woman, the kind who has lived in you always.

Your past has no business defining your future, sis.

Take your journal out and do me a couple of favors.

Picture you. Not you with a million dollars and thousands of followers. Just you. Your favorite outfit. Your environment. Who's around you. What you're listening to. And what you feel. Go into as much detail as possible.

Your authentic you is your biggest role model. Now tell me what serves her. Close your eyes and just be an observer of your thoughts, and now picture what you wrote. Breathe it all in and exhale onto paper all the beautiful things that serve her.

Meditate on that vision. On what serves you, how enough you are, and that you can heal however you want for as long as you want.

Rip out this paper you wrote. Put it in your wallet, on your dashboard, wherever. Let it be a little love note to yourself to remind you how enough you are.

CHAPTER FIVE

THE CHOICES WE MAKE

By Addie Elizabeth Vega

"You must take personal responsibility. You cannot change the circumstances, the seasons, or the wind, but you can change yourself." - Jim Rohn

Well, here it is. I have five days until the deadline, and I am literally just starting to write this chapter for you all. It's not like I waited until the very last minute. I have notes everywhere; the back of bank deposit slips, receipts, post-its, you name it. Each one contains different ideas on which way I wanted to go with sharing my story. In 500-2000 words, I am supposed to share with you something I struggled with and the strategy I used to survive. Seriously? I could go on for a year straight.

And anyone that knows me knows I really can talk for that long.

The truth is we all face struggles. We all have adversities that challenge us, and situations or circumstances that bring us to our knees until we are screaming at the top of our lungs that we yield, only to have those desperate words fall on deaf ears. You feel helpless. It feels hopeless. Do not be deceived because NO ONE is exempt. We all have some trauma that has shaken us to our core. While we are in it, we stumble and fall, and have to get back up again and again. It's there, in the falling and getting up, that we grow. We change and are forced to shift perspectives in order to see another way. And with grit and determination, we refuse to stay down. We use faith and the littlest of gratitudes to fuel us in rebuilding ourselves back up from the shattered ground beneath our feet. It's in these words I share with you how my apparent "failures" became my greatest teachers and ultimately tremendous gifts. And the same is true for you.

My mother was the rock of our family. She was truly an amazing woman. So much of who I am is attributed to her. She passed from terminal brain cancer in 2016. I was supposed to start medical school the week after we found out about her brain cancer. That same year, I faced financial hardship (I had stayed home, and my siblings and I helped to care for my mother's end of life), my 21-year relationship with my husband ended the following year. Nothing in my life looked anything like it had before my mother's diagnosis. The heartbreak was unbearable. I had no clue what direction I was going in. Throw grief in there, and I had become utterly paralyzed. "It's normal," they said. "It's all part of the process." They made it seem like it was supposed to be a tremendous relief that I was meeting statistical standards on how one should feel after enduring total world destruction. But I had to function! I couldn't wash my hair without napping before AND after. It took all my energy to walk out of the house without having a panic attack. I literally felt like the world was caving in on me. And I had to work and support two children who were equally as broken. Should I throw in during that same hellish time period that our dog died, we sold their childhood home and they both had to switch schools? Their tears absolutely destroyed me. I couldn't fix it. I couldn't change it. I felt like I had failed them. Failed at every single thing I had been working so hard to hold together for so many years.

It was one of the hardest yet most transformative experiences of my life. I want to share every sordid detail. Every miserable thing that happened. I want to finally let it out and have someone understand just how dire my circumstances were. I'm sure we could compare stories on all the pain, all the bullshit moves and lies from our exes, but now, I realize that isn't the part that counts. One day, when I was speaking with my sister Chelsie, she said, "Sister, I love you and have been listening to you complaining for months about your circumstances, but you have changed nothing. I feel like I'm not helping you. I'm enabling you. I'm always here for you, but unless you are talking about actions you are taking in another direction, I can't listen to this anymore."

I was so hurt at first, but it was in her words that I realized she was right! It isn't until YOU change YOUR story that your circumstances will change. You have to change your mind about the matter, you have to believe you can and then you have to do it. So that is what I did. I thought for sure I would die at first. So, I surrendered. I said, "God, if today is the day you decide to take me, so be it, but I am going to carry on with my business until I hit the ground." And I did. I made a choice to have my faith be bigger than my fear. I called it "blind faith" because I certainly did not see a way forward. Instead, I just kept putting one foot in front of the other and prayed like crazy for Jesus to take the wheel. I got up, got dressed like I was going into work every single day, and when things were really hard, I would wear red lipstick.

Red signifies strength, courage, and confidence to me. I also had a perfume I would always wear. I told myself that as long as I was wearing it, I could make it through anything. Find something that makes you feel strong! I took pictures all day long, being mindful, and finding gratitude in everything. At the end of even the most challenging day, I would lay in bed, look back at the moments I had with my girls, or while I was walking outside or doing something I loved, and I was able to sleep again. I was going to bed with my heart full of love and gratitude instead of worry and stress. I did this every night and still do to this day. There are so many fleeting moments that seem so insignificant, but I learned that after my mother passed, and now three years later missing her more than ever, no moments are insignificant. They all matter. You must choose to follow the flow of the people, places, and things that inspire you, not exhaust you. So, slow down and be choosy. Don't leave your living experience to chance!

It may seem silly but it worked for me. It's the little things that have the most significant impact. Start small. Baby steps. I practiced mirror work and wrote out mantras on flashcards or on my hand. It was critical for both my mental and physical health to create some movement. I could barely walk for ten minutes without a three-day recovery, but I kept going. I practiced restorative yoga, modified my food choices and daily habits. I went back to school. Learning new things got me out of my head. It forced me to use my brain instead of it running on autopilot with obsessive thoughts. Learning new information broke the cycle. I had no money. So, I found free classes on anything that sparked an interest. YouTube is a great source of inspiration! I love Les Brown, Louise Hay, Mel Robbins, Oprah, Rachel Hollis, Jack Canfield. There is SO much out there for you, so use it! The healing truly begins with making a choice to lean in and learn to love and care for yourself. And for me, it had been a very long time since I had given that any attention.

Life is full of waves. My siblings and I refer to them as "ebbs and flows." It's part of life. It's living. The value lies in the choices we make in response to our hardships. There is no love without loss. There is no trying without failing. So, do we not love? Do we not try? The living is in the effort. It's the ups, the downs, the in-betweens. There are many variables between us all. We all come from different backgrounds, have different educations, different financial situations, but at the end of the day, there is one thing we all have in common: We all have the capability to choose. Before all of this, I was just existing. I lived my life from a place of fear, trying to keep my precariously built house of cards from collapsing. I see that now. But it doesn't work. Life is here to be lived. So, choose to live. Make a commitment to yourself every day. Do it with gusto! We can choose to live a better life, to heal, to get up, to get dressed. My goal was 1% better every day. Anyone can do that! It's achievable. Set small goals and plan to fall. Because you will. But you will get up, and each time you do, you will be a little stronger. I have grown SO much from realizing that good, bad or indifferent, it is MY choices that ultimately lead me where I want to go, and you can do it, too!

And don't for one second think you don't matter. You do. YOU. MATTER. If anyone tells you otherwise, tell them to pound sand! You are worth making better choices for yourself. Fear will tell you you'll fail, that you aren't worthy, that there is no other way, that you're not strong enough. And faith, at first, may be barely audible. It is that teeny tiny voice you can scarcely hear on the other side of your tears. When the well is dry and there is not a drop left, that little spark of life speaks up. It's the one that says, "Lean in. It's time to get up." And I implore you, no matter how shakey your legs feel or how bad your hands tremble, get up! You have to take 100% responsibility for your life. No buts. No blaming. No excuses. We all have a million different reasons why we stay at a job we hate, why we stay in a relationship that utterly deflates us, why we continue to make poor food choices, why we don't listen to our intuition. The list goes on. You fill in the blank. But the reality is that by choosing not to make a change, you are still making a choice. Insanity is doing the same thing over and over and expecting a different result. Now is the time to change your response. Stop being a victim of your circumstances. Scream in the face of fear and choose to take steps toward a life that is worth living! If you want life to look different, you need to choose differently, and this starts with the way you think. So, start by thinking that instead of things happening *to* you they are happening *for* you. You got this!

It's time to step into who you were meant to be. The events that occur in our lives, whether they're good, bad, or indifferent, are all part of the process. When the hard stuff happens, and our hearts shatter and we feel defeated, it is okay to feel those emotions. You are supposed to feel those emotions! Despite what all those smiling faces on social media are posting, they all feel pain, too. No one is exempt. No one. So, feel them. Embrace them. You are strong. You are brave. You can. You really can. And you must! What are your alternatives? I used something my mother always said to me when I literally felt I simply could not face certain challenges. She would say, "You can, you will, and you're gonna." She would say it with such conviction like she knew it to be true because she believed in me. She could see it was a time I didn't believe in myself. And the real kicker was when she said, "You're gonna" in the tone moms love to use when they want you to move your ass or face the consequences. It was a non-option. Just get it done. And that is what I did. I said it over and over. She isn't here to share those words with me anymore, but they are so ingrained that I can hear her as if she were. It's funny the things we cherish once people are gone. Unfortunately, sometimes it's not until people are truly gone that we finally grasp what they were trying to tell us all along.

It doesn't matter where you are, how much money you have, or what you have done because you matter. And you are here for a reason. Know this and embrace it. As my dad loves to say, when things get hard, "Stay the course." Let your light shine. You never know how far that light may shine on someone else! Switch that mindset from a place of fear to one of unwavering faith. It will get you through most anything. I know it is scary. I know you feel like you can't. But I promise you can! So, lean in. Take risks. Surrender to things you cannot control, and control the things you can. Hm, have you heard that somewhere before?

As Mel Robbins says, "5-4-3-2-1."

Let's go!

CHAPTER SIX

FINDING THE COURAGE TO LEAVE

By Kaylie Pierre

As I took my eyes off my screaming husband and looked past him, I saw my three little kiddos sitting on the floor watching their daddy yell at their mommy. At that moment, I knew two things: I could not live like this anymore, and I absolutely could not let my kids see this happen again.

I want to share with you the story of how I found the courage to leave my toxic marriage and start a new life as a single mom of three kids. Finding the courage to leave was overwhelmingly scary, but the truth is that leaving was the best thing I could have done for myself and my kids.

My husband and I were those crazy people who got married

way too fast, but we were so in love and couldn't wait to start our lives together. We had the most perfect little wedding done our way, with just four of our closest friends there to witness us promise to spend the rest of our lives together. It was beautiful.

The first year we were together, things were wonderful. We got married, we bought a car together, we moved into a house together and a few months after we got married, I was pregnant with twins. He was my best friend, we laughed together, had silly jokes, and shared our hopes and dreams for our future family. I felt like I was getting my fairy tale ending. As cheesy as that sounds, everything was absolutely amazing.

When I was seven months pregnant with my twins, I got my first glimpse of how scary my husband could be. He had gotten on my Facebook and found old messages between myself and a friend where I was talking about another guy who I had met prior to meeting my husband. These messages ignited a rage inside my husband that I had no clue existed. I had no idea he was capable of screaming that way. The anger in his eyes terrified me so much that I felt my fight or flight instincts kick in telling me, "This is not okay. You aren't safe." I didn't know what to do, so I hid in our walk-in closet, crying hysterically on the floor, holding onto my babies inside my belly. I remember trying to talk to my babies, telling them everything was okay, but they knew it wasn't. They could feel my muscles contracting around them. It wasn't long until my husband found me and unsympathetically told me to get off the floor. I got up, went into our guest room, and locked the door behind me. I sat on the bed and cried as he continued to scream at me through the door. I remember thinking that maybe if I scream, the neighbors will hear me, and then I heard glass shatter. He had punched a mirror in the hall.

The blood dripping from his hand snapped him out of his rage. His voice was normal again, and although I was still scared, I unlocked the door and helped him stop the bleeding.

I was in shock, I couldn't believe I was seeing such a scary side of him that I hadn't known existed. Of course he apologized, he promised it wouldn't happen again and I believed him. The next day, we had our baby shower for our twins: We were surrounded by friends and family, and I didn't say a word. I was afraid to tell anyone what had happened, but I also felt an immense amount of shame for marrying a man who could be so awful to me. I decided it was better to not say anything because I didn't want anyone judging my husband.

After that day, life went back to normal, but that experience left an impression on me that I wouldn't forget or truly heal from. However, I believed so strongly in our marriage vows, and we were about to have twins, that I couldn't fathom any option other than moving forward. Life was good for nearly a year and a half. At this point, we had our beautiful twins and baby number three on the way! I was a work-from-home mom with twin toddlers, a baby on the way, and I was also doing the cooking, cleaning, grocery shopping, and laundry. I did it all. I was constantly on the verge of tears from exhaustion and feeling overwhelmed.

My husband traveled for work a few times a year. One evening, he got back from a trip, and while he relaxed, I made dinner, cleaned up the house, and started a bath for the twins. I had no idea he was about to go off on me again.

He started screaming at me. He was mad I didn't get off the couch to hug him when he got home. I was baffled that he was so mad about this. I was pregnant, exhausted and I had spent several days single parenting. Truthfully, the thought of greeting him with open arms and excitement hadn't even crossed my mind. Instead of letting my emotions get a hold of me, I tried to ignore him and focus on my two babies in the tub. I was faking a smile at them as I reassured them everything was okay.

At the time, we lived in a house where a single man rented the basement. I remember desperately praying he could hear my husband screaming at me and that he would come to help me, but he didn't. I started to panic. My husband was getting louder and scarier. He got in my face, and I remember thinking, "Is he really going to hit a pregnant woman with his two kids watching?"

I needed to do something, so I said, "I do not feel safe around you. You need to leave now, or I'm calling the cops." I had to repeat it several times before he took me seriously and left the house. I think he went for a walk. I felt so ashamed and guilty that my sweet babies had to witness it. That night, I slept in my twins' room because there was no way I could sleep next to him if and when he returned.

After that incident, I decided to visit my mom to get away for a bit. She lived a few hours away, and I needed some space to clear my head. Once again, my husband apologized for his behavior, but this time, I wasn't in as much denial, and I was ready to acknowledge this wasn't okay. I suggested we go to marriage counseling, and his response was, "I don't need someone to tell me how to be married to my wife," but

I refused to come home until he agreed to go. When I returned home, things were okay, and I prayed that marriage counseling would help us keep our family together. For a while, everything was okay again, but those two fights stuck with me and made me feel like I was constantly walking on eggshells, fearful I'd make him mad.

When baby number three was born, I found myself even more overwhelmed and exhausted with being a mom, still maintaining all the household duties and working from home. We even hired a part-time nanny, but emotionally and mentally, I was struggling. I constantly felt like I was on the verge of a breakdown, and my husband would get annoyed with me when I tried to tell him I wasn't okay, which left me feeling unsupported and unappreciated. I was too embarrassed to tell people how unhelpful he was, so I did my best to keep powering through the days with a fake smile and constantly telling people the lie that things were great for us.

As the months went by, I became resentful of my husband. It hurt me that he belittled my concerns for my well-being and showed no sympathy toward me, the woman he had married, and the mother of his kids. I avoided my husband as much as possible, and he did the same to me. We would go through the days barely talking, and I would often sleep with my kids in their room because I couldn't stand sleeping next to him.

On the night of our twins' third birthday, everything came to a head. Things started out as a fight we've had many times before: I felt unsupported and unappreciated, and he wanted love and affection. He couldn't understand why I had distanced myself from him. He once again belittled my cry for help and the fact that I was overwhelmed, exhausted, and struggling with my well-being. All I wanted was the support from my husband. He said terrible, awful things to me, things a husband should never say to a wife, and although I think we were both feeling things that are normal for parents with young kiddos, the unhealthy communication and negative feelings toward each other destroyed our marriage and created a toxic environment I desperately wanted out of.

And that brings us back to the beginning of this chapter: the moment I decided I couldn't do this anymore. The moment I decided I was done. As he continued to scream in my face, I leaned back over the kitchen counter to create space between us, and once again found myself telling him I was going to call the police if he didn't leave. Eventually, he got in his car and left. While he was gone, I started planning my escape. I called my sister and told her what was going on. I told her I needed to leave and that I wasn't coming back. I reached out to a friend on Facebook who was the only person I could think of who was my age and divorced, and I asked her for advice.

I started getting the kids ready for bed when my husband returned home, I texted my sister and said, "Please don't call or text me. He's home, and I don't want him to know what's going on." She responded to ask if I was okay, and I said, "Yes. Please don't let me chicken out. I'm leaving tomorrow." I cleared out my text messages and went to bed next to my husband with my phone under my pillow, absolutely terrified.

The next day, shortly after my husband left for work, our nanny arrived. I asked her to help me pack up because I was leaving, and bless her heart, she did. In less than an hour, my minivan was full of garbage bags and laundry baskets with everything I could grab for my kids and myself. As I backed out of my driveway and put the car in drive, I felt a weight lifted off my shoulders. I was free, and I wasn't going back.

Finding the courage to leave was the scariest thing I'd ever done, but the only thing scarier than leaving was staying in a toxic relationship and raising my kids in a home where their mother feared their father. I knew I deserved better, and my kids absolutely deserved to grow up in a happy and healthy environment. As their mother, it's my responsibility to give them that.

I left my husband almost a year and a half ago, and I can say I'm happier than I've ever been. Yes, being a single mom is challenging, but truthfully, in many ways, it's easier because I'm no longer being emotionally drained from a marriage that didn't serve me. Finding the courage to leave was terrifying, but it was also the most empowering and bravest thing I've ever done for myself and my kids.

CHAPTER SEVEN

A CHOICE FOR MOTHERLESS MOTHERS

By Melissa J. Erskine

O ften, it seems, I'm alone in being a motherless mother. I inwardly cringe when I'm at work or in other social situations while around other parents who don't know my background and casually mention how their mother helped them with x, y, or z as they became a mother themselves. The loneliness and ache blooms in my belly, and I feel the profound loss of not having had my mother alive when my first child was born.

Our mourning never really ceases. Mine never has, but the pain has lessened over time. There is a uniqueness to this grief that unleashes itself as if brand new on the day you give birth. As you make the transformation from daughter to mother, there is an expectation that your own mother will be there to help transition and support you in the role she's been working on since giving birth herself.

Having your own mother around when you give birth, or so I would think, is like having a person that reminds you to take care of yourself first and provides you with additional support. Those first months with a newborn completely eradicates any sense of who you once were. Between sleep deprivation, feedings, and caretaking in general, it makes it damn near impossible to figure out who you are now post-birth.

Without having the physical ambassador of my mother to remind me that, in order to be the best in all the roles I perform, especially that of a mother, I must put the oxygen mask on myself first. I found, not until after the birth of my second child, that the best way to do that is to get quiet, be still, and bring consciousness to the internal guidance and compass from within my own being through meditation.

My Mother

My mom was a myriad of things: an artist, a nurse, a woman of faith, funny, strong, a good friend, the rock, and center spoke of connection within our nuclear and extended families. She was also not a lot of things: overly sentimental, affectionate in words or physical form, and open about being angry or hurt.

She was first diagnosed with cancer in 2001 and battled it off and on for the next ten years. During this time, I witnessed her courage, her strength, and her strong will because she never stopped fighting. Rather than give in to the initial bleak diagnosis, she did what needed to be done to keep living. She wasn't allowing a diagnosis to tell her when her life was done.

She eventually had to have a colostomy bag attached, and even then, when some people would have allowed that to stop them from engaging in outside social situations, she found some fashionable cute bag to disguise her equipment. She refused to be hermetic about her changing physical body. No matter what the obstacle or obstruction, she gracefully added it to her life and kept moving. She didn't indulge in self-pity.

She emulated something else that became one of the legacies she left for me after she passed. After so many trials and tribulations throughout her life, my mother figured out something and modeled it in her later years: self-care comes first. After self-care, you can then tend to everyone else's needs. She did this through her devout Catholicism, going on women-only retreat weekends, and through her art. I am one of five children, and she could have easily given all of herself away to mother us, but she didn't. The resurgence of this lesson would come back to me, years after her death, and six months postpartum with the birth of my second child.

Finding My Own Oxygen Mask

Motherhood can be a lonely job. I clearly remember six months after my second child was born feeling completely worn thin. I couldn't remember the last time I had done something for myself or about myself that didn't in some way relate back to caring for everyone else. I didn't know who I was anymore, and I had forgotten what I enjoyed in the swirl of the nonstop repetition of the "You're Welcome" song from *Moana* and "Try Everything" from *Zootopia*.

I was impatient, tired, and resentful. I found myself focusing on regrets of the past and thinking of different scenarios for the future that weren't here yet or which I could not plan for. Mostly, I felt ashamed of the shell of the person I had become. I didn't want to miss out on these young years with my children in the void of despair or "future tripping." You know, being anywhere but in the present moment with my family. What could I do, I wondered. How do I find the time?

And the rollercoaster of cannot, shouldn't, or alternative excuses swirled through my brain.

There was a morning, sometime in November 2017, when I felt completely broken. It was in that brokenness that I swore I could hear my mother's voice, somewhat faded, as she said, "You need to take care of yourself first."

But what does that mean? Isn't that selfish? Self-centered? I thought about her again and the ways she practiced self-care before that was a trendy term. She fed her soul, her creativity, and herself through modalities that worked for her to give her own being life again before she could help anyone else.

Reflecting on this, I asked myself what self-care would mean for me. I also realized self-care isn't at all selfish. In fact, it is just the opposite. Strong, centered, clear in who and what you are, is one of the most positive models we can show our children. I thought about all the times I read about meditation, as well as all the times I tried it but never stuck to it.

From that day forward, I committed to creating a morning ritual for myself. I would get up before anyone else, be in the quiet of the early morning, and meditate.

Self-Care is Paramount to Being the Best Mother

You Can Be

With time, this morning ritual I created for myself became as important as sleeping, eating and breathing. My morning ritual has created a huge sense of empowerment I never thought I could possess but that I now realize is needed as a motherless mother. These moments of self-reflection have given me a clearer mind, allowing me to embrace the reality that, although I can't defer to my own mother for her wisdom and insight, I can work on keeping my mom alive. I will continue her legacy by passing on her understanding that self-love can awaken us to the greatest parts of ourselves and radiate them to those around us.

Through my meditation practice, I realize now that being a motherless mother has equipped me to become stronger and wiser by building my own experience and knowledge. I have found the self-confidence to tap into an innate and instinctual ability to know what is best for my kids. I can reassure myself that when I've cleared a space to be grounded and peaceful, they're happier and more peaceful, too.

I have learned to appreciate the present realities of my life when faced with less-than-ideal circumstances. I have become a more confident parent and feel more empowered with the insight to see a more enriched version of myself. I love myself and have proven that committing a couple of hours a day to my morning ritual has had profound effects on my own well-being, how I parent, and how I show up in the world.

In Conclusion

Although being a motherless mother puts you in a club you probably never wanted to join, it also gives us the unique strength to create forms of support for the toughest job you'll ever have. I truly believe that had I not been given the experience of giving birth and raising my children without my mother around, I would not have come to the lifeline of meditation and mindfulness. What may feel like a luxury to some is a necessity for me.

Without the help of a living maternal guide, you can become your own guide. Create rituals and practices to connect to that wisdom in your soul and the DNA stamp of your mother that birthed you.

Even if you're a mom with your own mom still around, I encourage you to try the following meditation every morning for a month. It takes thirty days to reliably form a new habit, and I can promise you this will be one of the healthiest and kindest habits you can do for yourself.

Loving Kindness Meditation:

- Sit comfortably. Any position will do. Close your eyes and take a few deep breaths. Inhale and exhale slowly. Consciously relax your muscles and prepare your body and mind for a deep awareness of love and compassion.

- Choose a person you love. Choose someone who you love easily and naturally rather than someone for whom you feel an emotionally complicated love.

- Focus on the area around your heart. Put your hand over your heart. Once you are able to focus on your heart, imagine breathing in and out through your heart. Take several deep breaths and feel your heart breathing.

- Turn your attention to feelings of gratitude and love, warm and tender, for the person you chose.

- Send Loving Kindness and Compassion to Yourself: Imagine the warm glow of love and compassion coming from your heart is moving throughout your body. Send these feelings up and down your body. If verbal content is easier for you to connect to, you can repeat the following words: "May I be happy. May I be well. May I be safe. May I be peaceful and at ease."

- Send Loving Kindness and Compassion to Family and Friends: Imagine friends and family as vividly as you can and send these feelings into their hearts. Imagine the warm glow of love and compassion that comes from your heart moving into their hearts. If verbal content is easier for you to connect to, you can repeat the following words: "May you be happy. May you be well. May you be safe. May you be peaceful and at ease."

- Expand the circle by sending your Loving Kindness and Compassion to neighbors, acquaintances, strangers, animals, and people with whom you have a difficult or complicated relationship.

- Imagine planet Earth, with all its inhabitants, and send Loving Kindness and Compassion to all living beings.

CHAPTER EIGHT
DEFINING MOMENTS

By Sharon Fulmer

"Choice is the most powerful tool we have. Everything boils down to our choices. We exist in a field of infinite possibilities." - Tiny Buddha

She was fifteen and full of joy, hope, and promise. Soon, a decision would be made for her that would thrust her into a world that would change her life forever. She went from fifteen in the prime of her life, to sixteen and pregnant, and at seventeen, she married an abusive husband. She stayed in the marriage for sixteen years before making a shift. We called her *Girl, Interrupted.*

In the next few lines, we'll talk about her life and how she survived it all.

In this life, you are responsible for your choices. You don't have to be an expert, you just have to live your life.

This story is about becoming self-reliant, making choices, and moving forward. In it, you will share her experiences and what her mother calls wit and wisdom.

It is my desire that, as you go on her journey, it will give you the desire needed to live a bigger and more fulfilled life.

We all come into this world with both blessings and curses. It is a blessing to be born alive and healthy, and the rest is debatable...

Who is she? She is various women:

She is your sixteen-year-old pregnant daughter, your abused sister, your battered wife, your mom afraid for her children, a secret keeper, the I-can't-really-tell-you-my-real-story friend.

She was hesitant about sharing her story. She didn't want to embarrass her family, but if she can save one woman from years of abuse and bad choices it's all worth it, so she's all in.

Never again can women go back to those dark times when we had no power at all. Never again shall we give up our right to choose.

Hardships and trials are part of our journey, but our trials have a purpose.

It's what you do, not what you say you will do, that matters.

This true story will show you how to make significant changes to a stagnant life or relationship. To learn how to put more value on yourself, ask for more out of life, and get it. To live the life you were born to live, you can do it with just one mind shift.

It's June, and she graduated from junior high, looking forward to summer and hanging out with her childhood friends. She also looked forward to starting the new year as a high schooler.

Imagine, if you will, it's fall and the leaves are turning yellow, red and a beautiful burnt orange.

It's lovely on the East Coast in October when the seasons change. It's her favorite time of year. She is excited to be in a new high school.

THEN, her life is interrupted. Her mom says they are moving to the West Coast. Her entire world as she knew it falls apart in one fell swoop and her dream is gone.

Her arrival at a new school was not well received. She had a thick East Coast accent. The boys in the new school thought she was just the greatest thing since sliced bread, with her long hair, coffee with lots of cream skin, shapely body, and that thick East Coast accent. They thought, *wow, something new*, but she was not very well-received by the young ladies. She had a few guy friends to chum around with, but no girlfriends. She was a year ahead of her class in the new school and a mature thinker. She had no interest in the boys at school at all. They were silly and immature.

It was a hot summer night and she was still fairly new to the city. It was that funky time of a girl's life at fifteen where she truly had no close friends. She was lonely and homesick for the friends and environment back east, so she decided to hang out with some new acquaintances, which included a guy that she thought was just all that and two bags of chips. He was older than her and had a nice car. She found herself in a situation that was foreign to her, as her new acquaintances were all older than her. She didn't want to stand out, so she just went along with the crowd, not really knowing what she was supposed to be doing.

She was fifteen and making choices that would affect the rest of her life. Two months after that adventurous night, she discovered she was pregnant. Her mother and father decided it would be best to send her to a school for pregnant teens. She would finish out the school year and return to her life, or so they said. At this maternity school/home, you are given the option to put your baby up for adoption or to keep your child. She never for one minute considered not bringing her baby home with her. Time passed and she gave birth to a beautiful baby girl.

Still living at home with her mom and completing high school, she made a choice to be better than what she was witnessing in society around her.

At seventeen, she got married, and for the first six months or so, the marriage was okay, but then reality struck. He was abusive. Once, he hit her so hard, her left eye was blackened, and before it could heal the following week, he hit her again and her right eye was also black. And still, she stayed trying to do what she thought was morally right by keeping her family together and hiding the abuse from other family members. For fifteen years, he abused her, either physically or verbally. And then that moment came when she made a shift.

"You may not control all the events that happen to you, but you can decide not to be reduced by them." -Maya Angelou

She was determined to have a career and be a great example to her daughter, so she finished high school and enrolled in the local junior college.

While attending college, she applied for a part-time position in the apparel industry as a receptionist. Intending to increase her salary, she made the decision to learn everything she could about the company and what they were manufacturing.

The manager was so impressed with her eagerness to learn that he offered her a promotion and a full-time position at the corporate office as a showroom sales representative. She was totally at home being a follower of fashion, so she accepted. Now she was playing in the bigger sandbox.

This opportunity introduced her to professional sales training and lots of domestic travel. She had arrived. Her husband was not at all pleased with the new position and the freedom it gave her, but she was determined not to be hindered by his jealousy and abuse.

I asked, "How did you do it? How did you survive an abusive marriage?"

Her answer: focus and being intentional. She focused on something bigger than herself, which was her children. Her intention was to make sure they didn't go through any more hard times.

She was tired of being abused every day, both verbally and physically. She was tired, so she made a decision. It was not so much for herself, but for her children. She had to leave. She would not continue to live that life and allow her children to believe it was normal. She wanted out.

And she did it. By planning her departure/escape, step-by-step, she focused only on the blessings she had, and not on what she was enduring. She focused on where she was about to go and not where she was.

That was the key: When you have something driving you forward, and you determine that you're worth more and want more, then you start to experience the shift.

Write it out: what you want, where you want to be, how you plan to achieve the desired results.

Maybe it's not happening for you right now, but you can do it. Don't dismiss the power of putting down your thoughts and desires. Transfer your thoughts to paper, as it will help you imagine the best way forward, and then work on them. Follow up every day, nurture them as if they were your children, grow them, and drive yourself toward them.

She determined that she was worthy of more and desired a

better life, so she left with three kids and no place to go.

She wrote in bullet points:

- What do I want?

- What tools do I need to achieve my desires?

- What actions are needed to get them?

- What is my time frame?

She started with small steps, like a one-bedroom apartment for herself and her children. During this time, she found another position in the apparel industry. With the sales training she had received, she was able to negotiate a better salary. Soon, she was able to get a three-bedroom house.

It took time to make the shift and find the silver lining to begin the journey.

She now chooses to empower women by coaching, speaking, and writing to end domestic violence and help others find their way to peace and happiness.

There is a line from the movie *Pretty Woman* where Richard Gere says to Julia Roberts, "I'm only going to keep you for six days, and then I will let you go", and she says, "But I'm here now."

That's how you must start to think: It doesn't matter that you may be let go; you're here now, so make the best of where you are right now. Just know that's not the end of your journey. Don't ever look back because you're not going that way.

How did she make the shift? She had a purpose. Her children, they saved her and gave her the strength she needed to keep moving forward. She hopes she made them proud and that her story would inspire and motivate you to find your purpose and make the decision to move forward.

I am your daughter who loves you so much, and I'm proud to be called your daughter. I am your sister who is doing awesome things, and I want to share them with you. I am no longer your wife and have learned to forgive you as well as myself.

I am your mom, who is no longer afraid but full of life and knowledge to share with you as you travel your road. I am your friend who can now be transparent. I can listen to your troubles, your successes, sit with you when you laugh, and hug you when you cry. I can hear your heart if you let me.

I am your grandmother keeping our history of strong women alive and adding some spice to it, moving forward, widening the path for you.

I am God's gift to all who will receive me. I am a woman working toward her dream.

No matter what your situation or obstacle is, a bad relationship or a horrible job, it can all change once you decide to make a mind shift and choose better.

You may not be there yet, but you are closer than you were yesterday!

CHAPTER NINE

TRANSFORMING LOSS INTO EMPOWERMENT

By Rachel Ali

You're at a place in your life you never thought you'd be. You may have lost your job and don't know how you'll pay rent. Maybe you're getting divorced. Perhaps you've moved back in with your parents in order to survive. Whatever your situation is, you may be resentful. Embarrassed. You may be angry. You hope you don't run into anyone you know when you're out and about because they'll ask what you've been up to and you don't want to explain why you're a total failure.

I'll never forget the morning I drove away from my home with just my daughters, three and six years old at the time. After almost eight years in an unhealthy marriage, I was walking away. I had waited quite some time. I knew this wasn't the example I wanted to set for my daughters regarding what a healthy relationship should look like. They were getting older and more aware of what was going on. So, I left. Left to find me again. Left so they could have an example of what is okay to accept from others and what is not. I also left financial security and stability. Left a good job. Left our home. Left with nothing but our clothes. I felt empowered and like a failure all at once. Hopeful, yet hopeless. It was a terrifying risk, moving back home with my parents, to the hometown I despised and thought I had left behind for good years before.

This is how I found happiness, and subsequently found success, amidst grief, fear, and the loss of everything I thought I needed, and how you can too.

For about two years after I left, I supported us with $11-$13 an hour and help here and there from family members who had hearts of gold. I had a bachelor's degree and an Esthetics License, but the job prospects were dim in the blue-collar town I grew up in. I felt stuck. Honestly, I didn't even know what I liked or didn't like, and I was flailing around trying to grasp anything that could give me a breath of air. This went on for almost a year. I reached a point where I was tired of being in my own head; unhappy and not knowing which direction to go in. I realized I was connecting my happiness purely to my financial status when, in reality, isn't happiness just a sense of fulfillment? Being financially secure definitely makes life easier, yes, but what about physical and mental health? Relationships? Spiritual life? Intellectual growth? Lucky us because there are so many facets of life, and there is ALWAYS something we can be planning, growing, and executing in one aspect or another. This way, no matter what is going on in one aspect, we can be attaining goals in another and thereby growing and feeling successful. As a perk, we are also building our self-worth, and creating a solid reason to get up every morning, which is vital after a set-back.

Step One: Have a Plan to Accomplish Your Goals, Steps for That Plan, and Micro-Goals for Those Steps

What type of woman do you envision yourself being? This could be anything and everything from where you would want to live, what you want to do for work, what income you strive for, what attributes are important to you, what music you listen to, what your hobbies are, etc. GET SPECIFIC. What do you like? This may be a hard question for those who sacrificed who they were for a long time, and it may take you some time to figure out. Write it all out and edit as you learn more about yourself. Once you figure out what your goals are and what you like, take steps to attain those goals. Your steps need to not only break down WHAT you want but HOW. Break the steps down into small and attainable parts. No matter how small the step, or as I like to call them, micro-goals, you're keeping small promises to yourself as you accomplish them, which means you're slowly but steadily rebuilding YOU.

Don't get overwhelmed by goals that are not currently workable. You ALWAYS have options. Work *with* life, not *against* it, and approach your goals with strategy. You can do this by optimizing what you currently have control over. It doesn't mean you have to give up on those goals currently "on standby." Instead, it means using your energy to grow and excel in those other areas. In addition, there may be micro-goals you can accomplish in the area you currently think you're stagnant in. You can always prepare yourself for your next move. If there are currently no promotional opportunities, but you know the job you would like to have requires A, B, and C, then get A, B, and C done so if the job opens up, you are fully qualified! For example, during the time when I felt I was financially "stuck," my main focus became my health and wellness. I still felt successful on a daily basis because I was setting and accomplishing goals in that area of my life. At the same time, I was living within my means, which contributed to my financial goals. Although I wasn't seeing tangible progress in that area at the time, it contributed to my overall success down the road. This requires research, time management, and planning on your part. Put the work into creating your life. No one cares more about your success than YOU. No one will hand you the keys to your dream life. Make the plans. Create micro-steps. Know what the steps are, and get them done, one by one. Remain flexible with what comes your way, and edit your steps accordingly. Keep moving forward for your future self.

Step Two: Self-Care

Once I hit that stride of fostering what I could control and not obsessing over what I couldn't, things started rolling. I began to focus on little things that contributed to my overall joy. Spending time outside with my girls, going on long walks with a friend, and physical health. My daughters would get involved sometimes, creating workouts for me or riding their bikes while I jogged. I was happy. Nothing had changed financially. I was still making $11/hour, but because I was accomplishing goals I had set for myself, and I was incorporating bits of joy into my everyday routine, I felt every day was an accomplishment. Oh, there were times when I would get a friendly reminder of my financial status. I had joined a well-known gym for $10/month, and one day, when I signed in at the desk, I was informed my payment hadn't gone through. I didn't even have $10 in my account. I went back to my car and cried for the hour I had allotted for gym time. I had been completely humiliated. We all have setbacks, but the key is to keep moving forward.

Health and well-being are the foundations of your life. If you're not well mentally and physically, that will spill over into every other aspect and goal in your life. Physical exertion not only relieves stress, but it also builds confidence and provides clarity and ideas for those goals you're working on. I've thought up some of my best ideas during particularly strenuous workouts, or maybe even during a walk! Your goal with fitness doesn't have to be to "look better." In actuality, I suggest that's NOT what you're striving for. Instead, focus on how it makes you feel. You probably want more energy, stress relief, self-confidence, and a routine built around self-love and self-improvement.

Another aspect of health and well-being is creating non-negotiables. You'll want to do these activities as often as possible so they contribute to your happiness. More often than not, these activities don't cost anything. They could be as simple as reading, cooking, journaling, listening to music or podcasts, photography, or laying in the sunshine and looking at the clouds (how many of us have done this since we were kids? It's amazing!). Whatever your "happy place" is, do more of that! Your soul needs it. Add specific happy goals or hobbies to your list so you can hold yourself accountable for doing them, as this is one of the easiest steps to push aside. This may be an area where you'd want to add in different therapeutic modalities as well, whether that's meditation, talk therapy, yoga, religious services, or whatever is needed to help you feel at peace during this time of growth.

Set boundaries. Who are you surrounding yourself with and what are you tolerating? You may find when you start putting yourself first, some of your friends or acquaintances may be unsupportive. If there are toxic people or naysayers in your life, people who think your goals are unattainable, or you're "not fun" anymore because you're spending your time differently, let them go.

Likewise, be mindful of asking advice from people who have no business giving it to you, or even asking questions you already know the answer to. In doing so, you're undermining your own value. If you catch yourself doing this, pay attention to how it makes you feel. Sometimes we subconsciously feed someone's ego and erode our own in the hopes of getting that person's approval or finding common ground. Even if it's something you truly don't know the answer to, try to find out the answer by doing your own research. This will increase your self-sufficiency and self-worth. If you're post-relationship and trying to find "you" again, asking for people's opinions on your endeavors will not help you find that. You've got to get deep, be introspective, and figure out who you are and where you stand. You drive your life; don't allow other people to. And when you DO need advice (as we all do at times), go to someone who has lived your circumstance.

Step Three: Execution

This is the scary part. It's not difficult (dare I say it's even fun?!) to create new goals for yourself, but now you have to act on them. It's not a question of *can* you, but *will* you? This is what sets you apart from everyone else. This is where the magic happens. People with less experience and talent than you may be wildly successful simply because they pressed the button. How often have you known people who say they're going to do this or that, and they never actually follow through? It's easy to talk yourself out of doing something because it's too hard and you're afraid to fail. Well, you'll definitely fail if you don't even try.

There are GREAT ideas out there that don't come to fruition due to lack of follow-through. The key here is **don't overthink it.** I sometimes get myself into "robot mode." This is not the time to be emotional: Save that for celebrating your successes. You've planned and worked hard to get to this point. It's easy to get in your feelings about it in order to justify not doing it. There are no feelings involved, to be honest. It's just something you need to do, something that you're going to do. Put your shoes on and go to the gym. Enroll in the class. Hit the "send" button. Accept that job that scares the shit out of you. Many things seem impossible until they're done, and pushing that button is what will get you to the point where you can look back and say, "I can't believe I did that. I've come so far."

Within a few months of getting my first decent paying job, another opportunity arose that would afford me a permanent full-time position with an increase in pay. It required public speaking. I was terrified of public speaking. If you had asked me years before if I would ever take a public speaking job, I would have said, "NEVER." But hard times give us a little extra backbone to push through fears, don't they? Isn't that great? I took the job. Since then, I have taken ANOTHER job with even MORE public speaking. If I had never been in the position I was in financially, I would have never pushed myself outside my comfort zone. I would have sat in contentment, not growing or evolving because it was "too scary." Take the risk. Challenge yourself. Do scary things. Now is the time.

Step Four: Remain Flexible

Always. This is an overarching theme to all the steps above, no matter what step you're on. Goals often don't go as planned, and this is no reason to feel defeated. Stop. Reevaluate. Create new steps. **Be flexible with what life hands you and move forward in conjunction with your opportunities.** Keep an open mind because sometimes something BETTER than what you could have ever imagined falls into your lap as a result of some crazy turn your life gave you! If ever your plans don't work out, always come back to this. If you feel overwhelmed by your micro-steps, simplify and simplify again until you're working on something attainable for you right now. It may be ONE very small goal. But you're moving forward, aren't you?

As time went on, I created a sense of self I'd never had before. My health was the best it had ever been, and I challenged myself in ways I would've never done had I not been forced to go through these growing pains. An increase in salary came with these changes EVEN THOUGH THAT WAS NOT MY MAIN FOCUS AT THE TIME. I now work as a recruiter, taking great pride in helping other women (and men) find meaningful, purpose-driven careers. I wouldn't be where I am today had I not gone through the painstaking evolution that forced me to face my situation head-on.

Challenges and obstacles will never stop being hurled at us. It's the game of life. Our path will never be straight or perfect. You will make progress. Maybe more progress than you ever dreamed. And yet all the while, more hurdles will rise up, and you may be pushed backward or to the left or right. This means you may need to reevaluate and edit your steps. This is a never-ending, ever-evolving process. By knowing the woman you want to be, creating micro-goals, making self-care a priority, executing your goals, and remaining flexible, you will look back and realize you can be happy and successful no matter what life throws at you. You may just end up in a place that's better than you ever could've imagined.

"A bird in a tree has no fear of the branch breaking because her trust rests not in the branch but in her own wings." - *Author Unknown*

CHAPTER TEN

THE JOURNEY BACK TO MYSELF

By Dr. Abby Reed

"Some seem to attract success, power, wealth, attainment with very little conscious effort: others conquer with great difficulty, still others fail altogether to reach their ambitions, desires, and ideals. Why is this so? The cause cannot be physical...hence the mind must be the creative force, must constitute the sole difference. It is the mind which overcomes the environment and every other obstacle." - Charles Haanel, The MasterKey System (1919)

A s I watched the hot pink cast being molded around my right hand, forearm, and up above my elbow, I knew my life was about to change drastically. This moment symbolized jumping off a cliff, into an abyss of the unknown, not knowing where I would land. You see, I am a chiropractor: My hands and the health of my body literally are the tools I use to perform my job. Receiving the news that I had severely broken my ulna on a vacation trip with my husband was not the life I had envisioned five months after starting my new practice in downtown Kansas City. And so, the broken arm-turned-spiritual journey of finding myself again had begun.

The first month after the injury was excruciatingly painful. I had never broken a bone, and the pain was deep, running through my whole body. I was unable to shower, dress, and do my hair. Applying makeup was like a cruel joke. My husband had to help me get ready. The first time he put my hair in a ridiculous looking ponytail, I both cried and laughed. The au natural look became my vibe for those four months. Daily tasks like cleaning, getting a glass of water, and driving was difficult and took double the time to perform. My life was full speed prior to this point; I had never felt weak or handicapped in my body until this moment in time, and so all of this was a huge adjustment.

While simple grooming was an arduous task, performing my job and being a doctor at my practice was impossible. The week before I broke my arm, I was seeing 80 patients per week. In the aftermath of my injury, we had to have another doctor take over my schedule as I healed. I went from 80 to 0 in a day, just like that. This season of my life turned into a four-month forced sabbatical, unintended and painful at the time, but in retrospect, it became the catalyst for true transformation and soul alignment in my life.

After several episodes of crying, feeling sorry for myself, asking God, the Universe, my angels and spirit guides why this all was happening, I got a download. Downloads are what I now refer to as direct messages from a higher power, with a whisper saying, "Trust me."

I stopped the internal battle and war within myself with that whisper and surrendered. I didn't know where my life or career was headed but I realized I could only control the controllable, and my only job at that point was to rest and to allow my body to heal. I had worked for eleven years attaining my education to become a doctor. I had been taking 30 hours of chiropractic school education and simultaneously working as a massage therapist on the weekends until I obtained my doctorate. The intensity then continued, as my first job out of chiropractic school was a two-hour commute a day. This was a time of pure grind. I was in hustle mode. The idea of rest was exotic and nonexistent in my life.

With the pink cast as my new fashion accessory, I began to ritualize slow medicine in the form of honoring my sleep, nurturing my body, and reading spiritual texts to create a more positive mindset. I had been void of inspiration in the time leading up to the arm break, as I was completely in adrenal fatigue and burnout. Slowing down provided a FLOOD of new ideas and vivid life experiences. While I was not able to adjust patients, I was able to perform acupuncture about eight weeks after the injury. To this day, I'm not sure how I was able to perform that with one arm, but with grace, I could re-establish that part of my practice.

One day, a friend and local fitness entrepreneur reached out because her mother and sisters were in town for a girl's day. They all wanted acupuncture appointments. Each of my treatments is an hour-long, and their overall appointment time was looking like 4+ hours. A millisecond of inspiration came in the form of an idea: Why not create a party experience, where they could all enjoy acupuncture together, in the comfort of their home? I had always been intrigued by the Real Housewives of Orange County's Botox parties, so why couldn't there be a healthy alternative party option for this kind of gathering? And so, Haven was created.

During that first party, the sun was shining into her loft as they were all enjoying being cozy under blankets on a huge sectional receiving acupuncture. The positive energy was palpable. After that experience, I created a business plan, took inspired action, and ordered blankets, acupuncture supplies, aromatherapy, and pillows in one day. The website and Instagram came next and then finding a graphic designer for our logo. We were live within a week and booked three parties for our first official launch day two weeks later. Haven, which eventually evolved into Sacred Chiropractic + Acupuncture a full -time health practice, is now over two years old and we have treated well over two thousand clients, from 12-year olds at a spa party, to a 50th birthday dinner party. We added mobile and virtual yoga to our services, created several retreats, have led yoga and acupuncture parties at several high-vibed gyms and opened a boutique wellness practice within a fully restored historical home in Kansas City.

It has been the most fulfilling and beautiful experience of my life as a healer and entrepreneur to see people be brave, get out of their comfort zones by trying this new form of medicine, and to create true community and memories through gathering. This all is nothing short of spirit working in my life, turning the devastating blow of my injury into something so sweet and soul-fulfilling. While the business took off and I was able to return to my full-time chiropractic practice months later, I still felt weak. My body would tire easily. I still felt foggy.

Before the accident, I was in the best shape of my life and had been working with a trainer. After the incident, it would take me 10 months to regain the stamina and motivation to return to the gym. My practice was growing, but not at the pace that I had envisioned. I knew the answer to uplevel was within me. I could feel a deep pool of unclaimed potential flowing just below the surface. Does that sound familiar? Going through what I have, I now know this energy resides in all of us and is waiting to manifest into your reality.

During this time, my husband was scaling a start-up technology company based out of Sydney, Australia. His job and the demands from it kept him going back and forth from the U.S. to Australia. While my entire life was centered around my career, I've always defined success as being a happy home. I would give up everything in my career to have a strong marriage and family life, as that has always been my number one priority. Over three hundred people around the world depended on my husband, and we accepted the job together as relative newlyweds, being married for only a year before he took the position. The job brought him ALIVE. He supported my practice building, and I knew I had a responsibility to support his dreams.

Every kiss goodbye before he would travel 4k miles to the other side of the world was heart-wrenching. It was literally like my beating heart was taken out of my body and placed on the other side of the world. His time zone was 17 hours ahead. On many days, if we talked on a Tuesday in the U.S., he was living in Wednesday in Australia. We joked and tried to make the best of his time travel and the hazy circumstances of our life during this time. I knew deep down, even more than ever, I needed to become stronger to be able to withstand the demands of my life at that time.

On New Year's Eve, 2018 going into 2019, I made a commitment to myself. I committed to becoming the strongest version of myself – body, mind, soul. The definition of strength is to have the ability to withstand great pressure or force. I had no choice: My life was beckoning me to uplevel, to handle with grace the pressure and the invitation to step into my full, unapologetic power sitting at my feet. And so, I began to run.

Growing up, my dad hosted a running club, and my earliest memories were Saturday morning 5k runs as a kid. I abandoned running altogether during my teenage and college years. In 2012, I decided to reconnect with my healthy roots and started the Couch to 5k app, running first in the Color Run. I remember the days of how excruciating it was to run just a minute at a time, but I kept going. I eventually ran my first half marathon in Boulder in 2015, the weekend I got engaged. It was the most empowering moment in my life, including graduating from chiropractic school at that time. Due to the practice building and my injury, I once again abandoned running. This call of my higher self to step back into my power beckoned me to revisit running.

So, without thinking, I signed up for a half marathon in Austin, the Zooma race series. Shape magazine had featured Zooma as one of the race series you should participate in as a woman, which instantly inspired me. I texted a couple of my best friends from around the country, and swiftly, Amber, Janae, and Rosanne and I were signed up and began training.

I frequently had to get comfortable with being uncomfortable during that time. We had committed to a race in the winter, and therefore, there were lots of outdoor cold runs. Before this experience, you wouldn't catch me outside if it was anything less than 50 degrees. And as the old Norwegian quote goes, there is no bad weather, just inadequate clothing, I began to realize that once bundled up, running outside was crazy refreshing. The cool air became my balm. Whenever I started to feel pain, I would remember the commitment I had made to myself, and that if I pushed a little more, a stronger version of myself would emerge.

We ran the Zooma women's race series in Austin the same weekend as South by Southwest, and the energy was electric. As I crossed the finish line while in pain, I felt a deep sense of satisfaction and inner strength well up within me. It was at that moment I decided while celebrating with a mimosa amongst my soul sisters and in a state of pure, happy exhaustion, I wasn't going to stop training.

For over a decade, I played with the idea of running a marathon. Even up until two years ago, I would have thought it was a completely unattainable goal. Sure, I had mentally gotten through the rigorous process of chiropractic school testing myself to my absolute limit intellectually, but a marathon? Physically, my mind could comprehend it. And now, knowing what I know, if something is planted in you, an idea so wild, so unfathomable, then it's a soul calling. Your higher self is whispering to you that whatever you dream up is within your capacity of achieving if you can learn the art of letting go of fear.

In yoga teacher training, one of the core foundational lessons is shifting fear-based thoughts to love-based thoughts. The fear-based thought is your ego. What we don't recognize at the moment is that it's an illusion: The fear is not real; it is our subconscious trying to stay safe and keep us in our comfort zone. Change and growth are scary for our egos. Once you become aware of it, you realize all those thoughts are limiting beliefs. The true secret to success in any area of your life is to feel fear, acknowledge it, and become aware that it is a limiting belief. Shedding light on your subconscious and stepping forward, despite the fear, is where true transformation happens. A life beyond your wildest dreams is on the other side of your fear.

What's something you have contemplated but held back from, for fear of the unknown? Your highest self and soul communicates directly with your body. You can tap into this ability anytime you are trying to decide to do something, especially when those actions bring up fear. It is very simple. Essentially, the moment you have a thought, do you expand or contract? The thoughts that give you a millisecond expansion are ones to follow and push past. It's a soul contract, inviting you to live up to your highest potential. I had that expansive moment thought with my marathon. The time was right. I had trained for a half marathon, completed it, and was in the mindset of seeing what my body and mind were capable of. My husband was still traveling to Australia, so I had time to commit to training. My brother and sister-in-law Aaron and Ann live in Paris, so I decided to couple my race with travel and pleasure visiting them abroad – a life hack I HIGHLY recommend. I decided to run my first trail marathon in Snowdonia National Park, in Wales, UK.

The Snowdonia Trail Marathon is a race that scales Wales' highest peak, Mt. Snowden. At mile 20, the course ascends 3500 feet to the summit. The mountain, in fact, is where many in the world go to train to scale Mt. Everest. The idea of the race scared the hell out of me, but under that fear was a deep, intoxicating pull of my intuition that told me it was the right race to train for. I had no idea if I could complete it, but I decided to try. That one decision changed my life.

I committed to a schedule of running daily, waking up with the sunrise to run trails in a forest behind my house. I signed up for several trail runs – the first in the Ozark Mountains in Missouri, a 16-miler race that took four hours to complete, and another 20-mile night race in the woods of Clinton Lake in Lawrence, KS.

Nighthawk, the night race, ended up being the first time I had water intoxication, which is when your body has an imbalance of electrolytes. This can be deadly. The run was in June on a 95-degree evening with a high percentage of humidity. This race was designed in my training plan to be the last long race before my full marathon, which was three weeks out. I knew I had to test my body to the extremes in order to withstand the intensity of Mt. Snowden. Getting sick during the race ended up teaching me a great lesson about hydration, and so with every setback, I improved, cultivated my skills, and became stronger and wiser for my race and life in general. I never understood the beauty of running in a forest until this chapter in my life.

The sounds of the forest were a balm to my body, butterflies dancing along the trails reminded me of the small moments of magic every day, and the sun streaming through the forest were all so therapeutic. This forest bathing became my medicine; the running was just the byproduct. The silence of the trails would allow me to think and to process unresolved feelings and mental blocks from the past. I was truly able to let go of energetic weight no longer serving me. Inspiration flooded back in for my chiropractic and acupuncture businesses. I had a renewed sense of being and got to know myself again.

The years of hustling and beginning my practice had me in constant overdrive and in a state of overwork. I began to understand that breaking my arm was the universe's way of realigning me and taking me on a journey back to myself. The forced sabbatical and the process of coming back home to my soul was long, painful, and not pretty at times, but the end result was beautiful: It literally gave me a view on a mountaintop where I could see not only Wales but Britain and Ireland in the distance.

Moments like that, I learned, are so outside our capacity to fathom, but if you trust your nudges, your journey, and your setbacks, and believe you are stronger than it all, you'll live a life on a higher plane of being. On July 14, 2019, I scaled Mt. Snowden. The just over 27 miles to the summit and back to the Wales village of Llanberis took nine hours to complete.I met many trail angels along the way, perfectly planted along my journey to help me in just the way I needed them for encouragement here, a biscuit or a cookie for energy there. When I thought I could not go any further, a beautiful radiant 70-plus-year-old man running the race gave me hope that we were almost to the top of the mountain. Hikers cheered us on, and I ran the last 5 miles to the finish line with a perfect stranger from Manchester, UK who was attempting his first trail marathon himself.

It was the most physically painful experience I have ever had in my life, but I learned that while testing your limits, your mind is a powerful tool. When I wanted to give up, I remembered why I had wanted this experience in the first place. I remember my husband cheering me on, my brother and sister-in-law traveling to Wales and waiting nine hours to see me cross the finish line, my patients cheering me on back in Kansas City. I remembered the commitment I had made to find the strongest version of myself. And I did. Crossing the finish line was beautiful, peaceful, emotional, and spiritual. I recommend, if you are ever looking for a dose of inspiration, to go stand at the finish line of a marathon. You'll witness agony and triumph. It's a beautiful thing to experience, and you can use that moment and that energy in your life for whatever mountain or tasks that may seem insurmountable.

If you commit fully to the greatest version of yourself, you are going to get results no matter what stands before you. The amazing thing about all of this? Once I recovered after the marathon, my chiropractic practice soared and I was able to fully integrate Haven into our practice that we renamed Sacred, to acknowledge the spiritual part of healing. I finally got it: success is a mindset game. Simply, the marathon was expansive for me; it taught me I am capable of so much more than what I previously thought I could handle. My soul, when aligned with my mind and body, is limitless.

So, what is it for you? What is one area of your life beckoning to be expanded upon? What is something at 80 years old you would be proud to say you achieved, while you had the opportunity to do so? Is it a marathon, a book, a trip around the world, creating that non-profit that has been in the back of your head, going back to school, investing in your business to help it grow, creating a product, or webinar? What is waiting to be birthed from you? There is no better time to shapeshift and pivot than now. The world circumstances of 2020 have beckoned us all to get into complete alignment and to create a life of intention and meaning.

Look at your setbacks as soul pauses for mind, body, spiritual growth, and maturity. If you do the daily work on your mind, your body, and your soul through those soul pauses, like a slingshot temporarily held back, you'll be catapulted forward at transformative speed. Accelerated change can be painful in the process. Trust that everything is happening not against you but for you; your job is to surrender. Dance with pain and setback, welcome it, and step into your greatness, face, and identify whatever fears and limiting beliefs hold you back. Design a life of beauty, truth, and courage. Magic, abundance, soul expansion and awakening is just on the other side of your mountain.

Learn more about the Diamond Mind authors at diamondmindbook.com

Made in the USA
Middletown, DE
17 August 2021

46146641R00066